MW01221802

O PEN Q UESTIONS IN WORSHIP

Gordon Lathrop, Series Editor

What are the essentials of Christian worship?

Gordon Lathrop

Augsburg Fortress

PUBLISHERS

Minneapolis, Minnesota

CONTENTS

OPEN QUESTIONS IN WORSHIP
What are the essentials of Christian worship?

Copyright © 1994 Augsburg Fortress. All rights reserved. Except for brief quotations in critical articles or reviews, no part of this book may be reproduced in any manner without prior written permission from the publisher. Write to: Permissions, Augsburg Fortress, 426 S. Fifth St., Box 1209, Minneapolis, MN 55440-1209.

Scripture quotations, unless otherwise noted, are from the New Revised Standard Version Bible © 1989 Division of Christian Education of the National Council of the Churches of Christ in the United States of America. Used by permission.

Editors: Samuel Torvend, Kari Kloos
Cover and interior design: Ann Elliot Artz
Cover photo: Ann Elliot Artz, from the Church of Santa Fosca, Island of Torcello, Italy

Manufactured in the U.S.A.   10-27972

98   97   96   95   94   1   2   3   4   5

INTRODUCTION

In the pursuit of wisdom, nothing is so inviting as a genuinely open question. An open question is one which in its honesty does not threaten by encouraging diverse opinions. The problem is that such questions find it difficult to survive in a climate of passions that can surround things held by faith. Indeed, because worship lies close to the heart of faith—as its source and its point of return—open questions about worship can be discerned as divisive exercises rather than profound sources of renewal.

More than twenty-five years ago, the bishops of the Second Vatican Council dared to treat the church's worship—precious as it was to them— as a point of openness. Generations before, a small body of Lutherans in the Iowa Synod also suggested that there might be open questions regarding worship, "open" because there was fundamental agreement on essential matters.

This series of small books is an attempt by a generation of Lutheran and other Christian scholars, pastors, and musicians to engage again some of the important questions regarding worship while embracing the legitimate diversity of viewpoints which Christians have regarding worship. The questions posed and the discussion offered are as much a gift to the ecumenical church as they are an intramural symposium.

In our own day, when we hear of "worship wars," Saint Paul's stern warning should be invoked: "If you bite and devour one another, take care that you are not consumed by one another" (Gal. 5:15). Indeed, this series brings sound scholarship and pastoral experience to bear on passionate questions—not to divide, but to encourage rediscovery and new insight.

Let us listen to these voices. Let them be heard among Lutherans and other Christians who care for the life and mission of the church. It is the end of one millennium of faith in Christ and the beginning of another. What better time to think and study and pray on the mysteries of God?

Paul Nelson
Director for Worship
Evangelical Lutheran Church in America

What are the essentials of Christian worship?

Gordon Lathrop

W hat exactly do we *do* if we mean to enact Christian public worship? That is a critical question for us as we care about the clarity of the Christian faith in this needy time. Or, we may ask the question in greater detail: What things do we need? What words do we speak or sing? What patterns do we follow?

Of course, many of us do not usually ask such questions. When we engage in Christian worship, we do what this congregation or parish to which we belong "has always done." Well, not quite always. We know that. Rather, we do this current Sunday's particular version of a pattern of Christian worship which this congregation has *received*. In many churches the pattern has been written down with directions for action and words for speaking and singing. In other churches the pattern is just as apparent, though not written: The pastoral prayer or the "altar call" always has a certain place in the order of unfolding events. In both cases, the recurring elements of the service are the predominant characteristics we sense in worship. They always connect to our memory of other times we have gone to church. Then certain changing elements—the scripture reading for today, the names of the sick *this* week—are placed under a seemingly timeless pattern. Indeed, the repetition of patterned actions and words into which present details may be inserted means that Christians do "rituals," the name anthropologists use in their study of worship.

But these rituals, these patterns of actions and words which constitute worship, have developed differently in different Christian communions. What is it that makes it possible to be in a gathering which is not our own and recognize it as Christian? Even Christians who belong to the same communion may experience very great differences in the actions they conduct. What holds them together? Indeed, as Christianity finds itself in diverse cultural situations throughout the world, it seeks to find ways to let the historic faith come to expression in the words, music, gestures, and worldview of a particular culture. What, then, should be so inculturated?

In addition, many Christians have discovered that their neighbors have practically no memory of Christian worship, that they are coming fresh to Christian faith. To what essentials in Christian worship should they be introduced? What exactly do we do if we mean to enact Christian public worship?

We may answer this question for ourselves by simply pointing to the practice of our own church. We use *Lutheran Book of Worship* or the Roman Catholic Mass or the Book of Common Prayer or our own group's pattern for worship. But this disciplined practice, cherished as it may be, does not set us free from the question. We cannot simply insist on *our* discipline. Indeed, in sorting out the treasures of our own tradition and its diversity, we may find some knowledge of that which is truly essential.

Still, we might refuse this question altogether. Some people see Christianity as an *essentially* plural phenomenon, diverse from its very beginning, and they see any attempt to find the "essentially Christian" anything—including worship—to be at best a doomed undertaking, and at worst an act of ideological tyranny. From this point of view, there are no "essentials" of Christian worship. There are diverse practices that may be described, encouraged, personally chosen, or ignored, but they cannot be *united*.

People who care about Christian worship need to listen to this point of view. There can be a kind of care about "essentials" which pushes legitimate diversity aside, sometimes doing so for the sake of an illegitimate desire for uniformity. But these concerns do not nullify the primitive Christian interest in "unity in Christ" nor the New Testament assertion of the "one baptism" (Eph. 4:5) and of the "one body" which partakes of the "one bread" (1 Cor. 10:17; cf. 12:13). It is still possible to inquire about the essentials while welcoming a full diversity of worship practice. For there can also be a kind of embrace of diversity which refuses to face the question of unity, choosing rather to cleave only to that which belongs to *me* and to *my group*. Here we say, no. In the vision of the Revelation to John (21:22-27), the many nations, with all their diverse treasures, are flowing into *one* city, the city which has God and the Lamb at the center of its worship.

But other Christians have recently refused the question in another way. Arguing that there are no central Christian worship actions, they assert that what is essential to Christian worship is a Christian *idea*, God's mercy or justification by grace, for example. Thus, Christian worship may do *anything*—most especially, it may do anything that is recognizable and accessible to the unchurched, as long as it meets their needs—as long as it carries this idea.

Again, those who care about the health of Christian worship should pay attention to the passion for the "outsider" in this proposal. But *communal actions are not just neutral, capable of bearing any idea.* If a Christian worship service is very much like television entertainment in its format and style, one must seriously question whether any idea of God's grace, which might indeed be mentioned in the talk or in a song, will be communicated. One must seriously question whether any "idea" will be heard as strongly as will the values of the entertainment industry: the values of stardom and of a marketing response to human needs.

Christian faith is more than an "idea." *It is the encounter with the grace of God present in Jesus Christ, and it involves the encounter with those concrete, flesh-and-blood things which connect us to the flesh of Jesus.* Welcoming others must involve welcoming them to a real community and to communal action as well. The central symbolic actions which Christians do must surely be set out in accessible, hospitable love, but they cannot be dispensed with.

Then what are those symbolic actions?

There are many open questions in Christian worship. This series of studies is intended to explore some of them. Indeed, to call these questions "open" is to follow in one tradition which insists that not everything that is disputed or marked by diversity has to be settled uniformly in order for there to be Christian unity.

In the mid-nineteenth century, the Iowa Synod made this assertion. But it also asserted there were certain matters which were not open, essential matters of the doctrine and practice of the Christian faith. Thus, in order for us to pursue a variety of open questions, we must begin with this: What are the essentials of Christian worship?

The ecumenical core

Many Christians in our day have dared to answer this question in increasing convergence with each other. One of the most significant statements on Christian unity in modern times, the World Council of Churches document *Baptism, Eucharist & Ministry*, makes clear by its title the central matters of worship: the water-bath we call baptism and the meal we call by many names. According to the same document, the ministry is able to carry out its chief responsibility "to assemble and build up the body of Christ" principally "by proclaiming and teaching the Word of God, by celebrating the sacraments, and by guiding the life of the community" (*BEM:* "Ministry," 13).

Many Christians use the phrase *word and sacrament* as shorthand for what they believe are the essentials of the Christian assembly. Thus the United Methodist Church calls its basic Sunday service "A Service of Word and Table" (*Book of Worship*, 1992, pp. 33-80). The Roman Catholic Church makes this assertion in what many consider to be the key passage of the *Constitution on the Sacred Liturgy*, one of the most important results of the movement for liturgical renewal in the twentieth century. The document states that Christ is present in the church in the *sacraments*, especially baptism and eucharist; in his *word*: "since it is he himself who speaks when the holy Scriptures are read in the Church"; and in the *gathering of the church* "for he promised: 'Where two or three are gathered together in my name, there am I in the midst of them' " (*Constitution on the Sacred Liturgy*, 7).

Indeed, many of us have been finding a new clarity of "word and sacrament" in our churches. That is, we find a new accent on scripture reading in harmony with other Christians using a common lectionary, a new sense of the importance of celebrating baptism in the midst of the community, and a continued growth in the frequency of the celebration of the supper.

We, too, may join this ecumenical company of Christians and assert that there are indeed essentials in Christian worship. These essentials are, quite simply, a community gathered around word and sacrament. Or, to say it more fully, they are **a participating community together with its ministers gathered on the Lord's Day in song and prayer around the scriptures, read and preached; around the baptismal washing, enacted or remembered; and around the holy supper.**

Lutherans have found authority for such an assertion in their central and classic confession concerning the church, presented in Augsburg in 1530:

> It is also taught among us that one holy Christian church will be and remain forever. This is the assembly of all believers among whom the gospel is preached in its purity and the holy sacraments are administered according to the gospel. For it is sufficient for the true unity of the Christian church that the gospel be preached in conformity with a pure understanding of it and that the sacraments be administered in accordance with the divine Word. It is not necessary for the true unity of the Christian church that ceremonies of human institution should be observed uniformly in all places. (*Augsburg Confession*, 7)

But while we may join these ecumenical voices and lay claim to this classic Lutheran witness, it remains for us to ask what "worship in word and sacrament" actually means. That is, first of all, why is it actually *these* things which are essential to Christian worship? *Is there any deeper meaning for us in their centrality than the sheer assertion that it is so?* Second, what actually *are* these things? *What is essential to doing them?* But now, for a moment, we should think more carefully about the reasons for *word and sacrament in a participating assembly* comprising the essentials of Christian worship.

Reference to word and sacrament, to their interaction and to their importance, can be found in many places besides official documents. The American Episcopalian Book of Common Prayer, for example, presents "An Order for Celebrating the Holy Eucharist" (pp. 400-401) which is its own list of the essentials of Christian worship. Interestingly, this list is a series of active verbs, making clear that these essentials are actions:

> The people and priest gather in the Lord's name, proclaim and respond to the word of God, pray for the world and the church, exchange the peace, prepare the table, make Eucharist, break the bread, share the gifts of God.

A similar sense of concrete, real actions was expressed on a simple nineteenth-century inscription found on the steeple bell of the Danish-American Lutheran parish church in Luck, Wisconsin:

> To the bath and the table,
> To the prayers and the word,
> I call every seeking soul.

But why the invitation to these simple things? Both the bell and the Book of Common Prayer seem silent, even mysterious, on these questions.

The Bible and the core

We come close to the deeper reasons when we look at the New Testament. To the extent that it is possible for us to ascertain, all the communities behind the New Testament writings treasure baptism as the way one enters the church. The reading of scripture as a liturgical practice is implied by passages in Luke, where the interpretation of scripture by the risen Lord is probably a model of the church's Sunday meeting (Luke 24:27,32,45; cf. 4:21); by passages in Paul, where the apostle's own letters are to be read in the gathered assembly (1 Thess. 5:27; Col. 4:16); and by the letters to the churches and the opening of the scroll in the Revelation to John (2–3; 5:1-10). Preaching is practiced everywhere. The Christian practice of the supper of the Lord is assumed by the "do this" of Luke (22:19) and Paul (1 Cor. 11:24-25), and by diverse reports in the New Testament. For example, that the meal is held every Sunday is reported of the community at Troas (Acts 20:7) and suggested by the first-day model of the Emmaus story: The risen Lord interprets the scriptures and is known in the blessing and sharing of the bread (Luke 24:30-31).

None of these passages give us great ceremonial detail about what the churches did when they gathered for worship. But this much is clear: In New Testament texts, the risen Christ bids the community *to teach and to baptize* (Matt. 28:19; cf. Mark 16:16), the Crucified and Risen One is known in *the explanation of scripture and in the meal* (Luke 24:30-32; cf. John 20:20; Rev. 5:6-7), and *preaching is full of the powerful weakness of the cross of Christ* (1 Cor. 1:17). These assertions of Christian faith underline the crucial significance of these central symbolic acts already among New Testament-era communities.

But these assertions also do more. They help us to see the deepest reason why the actions are essential: *They have to do with Jesus Christ.*

They do more, because in them we encounter the full reality of who Jesus is and what he does, and who we are as one body in Christ. There are certainly other things which some Christian communities did when they worshiped. But these things—baptism, preaching, the supper—are central to Christians because they have been seen as intimately bound up with who Christ is.

We see this connection of Jesus with those things that become the church's central actions already in the gospel traditions of his life. According to the Gospels, Jesus himself was *baptized* (Mark 1:9 and parallels). He himself came *preaching* (Mark 1:14 and parallels). And one of the ways he was most well known—even notorious—was by his constant *table-fellowship* with sinners (cf. Matt. 11:19; Luke 7:34). By this perspective, the church's gatherings around *these very things continue the actions of Jesus himself.*

We see the connection of Jesus Christ to the core actions of the church's worship even more strongly in the ongoing tradition of faith that *participation in these things is participation in him.* To be part of the community of word, baptism, and meal is to be gathered by the power of the Spirit into him, under the grace of the God who sent him.

The New Testament does not give us a constitution of the church nor a service book. It does give us Jesus Christ, seen and known amid ordinary things—water, words, a meal. Just as access to Christ would be difficult and skewed for us without the New Testament books, so also we need the concrete signs of water, communal words, and shared meal. Without them, when we speak of Jesus Christ we could easily be speaking more of ourselves than of the biblical, historic Christ. But with these living actions, we encounter the very *self* of Jesus breaking into any of our projected ideas: in the teaching, baptizing church, "I am with you always" (Matt. 28:20); the scriptures themselves "testify on my behalf" (John 5:39); in the meal, "this is my body" (Mark 14:22). These things are the concrete way of our encounter with his flesh, with him who is for us the revelation and the gift of God's grace.

Several important consequences follow from this deepest reason for the essential actions of Christian worship. In late twentieth-century North America, many people talk about Jesus Christ. That name is used for many religious ideas present in our culture—for self-realization plans, for politics, for ideas about the "soul" and about world-escape. Indeed, for some the name *Jesus* is a perfect synonym for popular American religion or, simply, for one's own self. More scholarly sorts assume that the only access to Jesus is through reconstructions of what he might have actually said or done. Such reconstructions are prey to the same pressures of current politics and religion, pressures now operative in the "reconstructor." But Christians have believed that who Jesus is and what he does are most reliably encountered in word and sacrament, that is, in the scriptures read next to that bath and that meal which are full of Jesus' own self-giving. But then we begin to see why these things are set out, according to the Luck bell, for "every seeking soul."

We might speculate about other possibilities, but we actually have no other means. These are the ones which are historically present in the New Testament and are found nearly universally in the life of the church. These concrete, real things connect us to him and to the real history of his body, the church.

They also connect us to the concrete, real earth. While we may say that we have these things simply because they are what actually comes to us from the culture in which Jesus was born and from the church's history, Christian faith has believed that *the universal availability of the stuff of these central symbols has been and is a gift from God.* Water is everywhere. Humans need it simply to live. Baptism is in any water, not some special or Near-Eastern water. Understandable but strongly symbolic speech, used to convey the deepest human values, is found in every culture. The oral witness to Jesus Christ can be made in that language and the Bible can be translated into it. Festive meals are found universally. The Lord's Supper is held with local bread and local wine—or, where these are simply not available or are far too expensive, with locally recognized staple food and festive drink—not with special, imported food. The things in which we encounter Jesus Christ are available everywhere. They are signs of the goodness of God's earth, as well as signs for the deep unity which God's mercy can establish between the good diversity of the many cultures of the world.

Furthermore, word, bath, and meal can be seen to be gifts which are inclusive in another sense. Words can be both praise and lament, the recounting of both death and life. Both are used in the stories of Israel and of Jesus, and both are welcome in the church. A bath can wash and a bath can drown. Both happen in the one use of water in the church. The joyful, life-giving meal of the community has the death of Jesus at the center of its memory and the dreadful hunger of our neighbors and of the world as the focus of our mission. The central things of Christian worship are not narrowly "religious" things nor are they concerned simply with happiness and success. *They welcome us to the full truth about ourselves: sorrow and hope, hunger and food, loneliness and community, sin and forgiveness, death and life. God in Christ comes amidst these things, full of mercy.*

But why all of these things? Would not just one be enough? No. The gift is more abundant than that. A set of words alone could easily be twisted into a list of things we have to do in order to be acceptable to God, unless it is constantly clear that *the content of the words is the same content which is washed over us in the bath and given to us to eat and drink in the supper.* Drinking the cup in which Christ says, "My blood, for you," gives us a key to understand the scriptures. Indeed, all preachers should strive to see that their sermons say in words the same thing that the bath and the cup say in actions. In the church, words should be edible, like bread, and just as full of grace. And the bread of Christ may be seen as a "word," one of the strongest words we have to speak the truth about God, the world, and ourselves. This is why, in the history of the Christian liturgy, the essential matters are always juxtaposed to each other and are always made up of at least two juxtaposed elements: readings *and* preaching, teaching *and* bathing, thanksgiving *and* receiving the food.

It then becomes clear that Christian communities and their leaders have a responsibility to let these things always *be* and *be seen to be* at the center of our gatherings. The word *worship* itself may mislead us into thinking that when we gather we may do anything which seems appropriate to us as "worship"—any sort of singing, any sort of "God-talk," any sort of exercise. But *if our gathering is about the grace of God in Jesus Christ, we cannot do without word and sacrament.* To pretend that "Christian freedom" includes freedom from these central things of Christ may be only to choose the bondage of our own opinions, our own religion, our own selves masquerading as God.

Yet, these essentials of Christian worship should not be seen as a burden. They are gifts and should be celebrated as gifts. Indeed, there can be various ways in which an assembly reads scripture and interprets it, washes those joining the community, and holds a meal. There can be many other secondary characteristics—musical style, architectural or artistic arrangement, patterns of entrance and leaving, leadership—which may make one assembly observing the central things seem very different from another.

But then what actually are these central things?

The prayers and the word

Christian worship includes scripture reading and preaching. It also includes prayers.

This assertion may be most clearly seen as true in the Christian Sunday or festival assembly, where scripture reading and preaching take a central role in almost all Christian communities. At other times, Christian communities may be remembering the Sunday readings and sermon or going toward them, and the presence of the word may be more subtle. A verse or two from the Sunday readings may be read as a summary. An additional biblical or nonbiblical text may be read that illuminates the Sunday readings. A hymn may be sung, echoing the Sunday readings. Or silence may be kept for the Sunday readings to keep on speaking.

But at the Sunday assembly the scripture is read. That means, *the book which is made up of the writings which have been recognized in the history of the church as authoritative and as appointed for public reading.* Indeed, the canon—the list of books in the Bible—is none other than the list of books which may be read in church. A bound Bible or lectionary belongs to the Christian assembly.

Why the Bible? Because Israel's stories set next to the stories from the earliest church make it possible for us to know the truth about the world's need and about God's grace in Jesus Christ. Because Jesus Christ is the living embodiment of all of God's scriptural promises. Because on the day of resurrection—and that is what Sunday is—the crucified and risen Lord interprets to us in all the scriptures the things concerning himself. So much is it so, that without such reading in the Sunday assembly, one may rightly doubt whether it is a Christian assembly at all.

Of course, Christians have some disagreement about the actual list of books which may be read. Roman Catholics include the ancient Jewish books which were only preserved in Greek, not Hebrew; Protestants do not. Episcopalians and some Lutherans hold a median position. They encourage the secondary reading of these books—the so-called Apocrypha— but discourage their use for the formation of doctrine. Yet, this minor disagreement should not distract us from the profound agreement: The biblical books are read so that Christ may be encountered. Indeed, Jerome articulated the universal faith of the church: "We eat the flesh and drink the blood of the divine Savior in the Holy Eucharist," said he, "but so do we in the reading of the scriptures."

It is then not as a book of history, moral lessons, or poetry that scripture is first of all read. It is read so that the community may encounter the truth about God in Jesus Christ enlivened by the living Spirit. It is read like the passage from Isaiah which Jesus read in the synagogue at Nazareth when he added: "Today this scripture has been fulfilled in your hearing" (Luke 4:21).

In fact, like the reading of the scriptures in the synagogue, in the time of Jesus, and in Jewish practice of the present day, the Sunday reading of the Bible in the Christian assembly is best made up of more than one reading. In the synagogue, the *torah* portion (a reading drawn from the first five books of the Bible, read according to a fixed annual or triennial cycle of selection) is followed by the *haftarah* ("completion"), which is a reading drawn from the rest of the Hebrew scriptures and chosen in relationship to the theme of the *torah* reading. This set of readings is then followed by interpretation through preaching, as Jesus did in the synagogue at Nazareth.

Since the earliest times in the church, there has been more than one reading set next to preaching. Justin, a lay Christian teacher of the second century church in Rome, wrote the clearest full description of the Christian Sunday assembly in about 150 C.E. The first part reads:

And on the day named after the sun all, whether they live in the city or the countryside, are gathered together in unity. Then the records of the apostles or the writings of the prophets are read for as long as there is time. When the reader has concluded, the presider in a discourse admonishes and invites us into the pattern of these good things. Then we all stand together and offer prayer. (1 *Apology*, 67)

But it is not simply because of the synagogue, the source for much Christian practice, nor because of the historical precedent in Christian circles that more than one reading is to be advised to Christians today, though these precedents should not be ignored or ridiculed. Rather, one passage set next to another, set next to yet another helps us to see both the fullness of God's gift and the sense that *it is not so much before the readings themselves as before the One whom they serve that we are gathered.* Indeed, Christians have understood *all* the readings in the assembly to be like the primary Christian metaphor for the four Gospel books: They are all, in their diversity, like the four great beasts of Ezekiel (1:5ff.) and of Revelation (4:6ff.) who gather around the throne of God and of the Lamb.

It is this understanding of the function of scripture in the assembly which has led to the development of the lectionary used by many Christian churches. While the use of such a collection of appointed readings is not an essential in Christian worship—as is the reading of scripture itself—a lectionary makes clear that the churches gather *together* before the word of God, as before a *gift*, and not that the churches or the preachers choose scripture passages according to their own moods or their own agendas or their own projections.

The current ecumenical three-year lectionary—widely used in Roman Catholic, Lutheran, Anglican, and Protestant churches—chooses a first reading from the Old Testament to relate to the theme of the third reading, drawn from one of the Gospels, rather like the synagogue *haftarah* was chosen in relationship to the *torah*. A reading from the letters of the New Testament is placed second, representing the churches which live from these scriptures. The risen Christ encountered in the Gospel reading— whom the assembly greets with acclamations like "Glory to you, O Lord!"— is then seen to be alive and present in *all* the readings. Such a gift from the tradition of Christian worship should not be lightly set aside. Those Christian assemblies who choose another manner of ordering their public reading of scripture should ask whether their manner as profoundly represents the Christian understanding of scripture, setting one text next to another around the living God and the Lamb.

In many churches these readings are surrounded by a pattern of song and action that makes the Christian use of the scriptures clear. Psalmody and hymnody place the biblical text in the mouth of the whole assembly, in forms appropriate to communal song. A psalm—often with a repeated refrain—may be used to receive and to meditate on the first reading. An "alleluia verse" may be used to greet the reading of the Gospel, the risen Christ being greeted with the old Hebrew word which Christians have long used for the celebration of the resurrection. The community may stand for this third reading, not because it is the most important reading, but because the story of Jesus, present now in the Gospel reading, is taken as the interpretative key to all the scriptures, like Jesus opening the ancient books to his disciples on the first Sunday (Luke 24).

But whether the lectionary is used or not, the scriptures are read at the Sunday meeting. At best, this reading will be at least one text set next to another, followed by *preaching*. Preaching, too, is an essential of Christian worship. What is essential is not a religious speech, certainly not a recitation of the current insights or experiences of the preacher. That preaching which belongs to the essentials of Christian worship is *a freely composed address, juxtaposed to the appointed readings, which opens up those readings to the assembly in such a way that their Christian intention is clear*. It will be a speech which articulates our utter need—using especially the images of the texts to do so—and articulates God's merciful presence in Christ. It will say in living words what the bath and the meal say in actions.

Thus, the "word" in the Christian assembly takes at least two forms: the classic written texts of scripture read aloud and the living voice of the preacher. These two forms are juxtaposed, even in a certain tension with each other. The texts always say more than the sermon can say, with an overflowing richness of meaning. Yet the sermon articulates the Christian purpose of reading the scriptures: that we may meet God's grace in Christ and trust it for our life. When preaching does not play this role, an essential element in Christian Sunday or festival worship is missing and the assembly is much diminished.

To make clear that this assembly around scripture and preaching is an assembly before *God*, the gathering is marked by prayer and hymnody or sung communal prayer. The classic western liturgy has come to mark the entrance into this service of readings and preaching with certain fixed songs (an entrance hymn, a litany and/or the Gloria) and with an opening prayer. But what is essential is not so much these particular elaborations as the sense that whatever is done must serve to gather us and give centrality to the reading of scripture.

The central matters are reading and preaching. But then these two forms press us to something more. They lead us to intercession for all the needs of church and world, and they invite us to the holy supper. Naming God's promises in the texts and preaching the One who is the fulfillment of God's promises awaken us to speak before God the names of many people in the world who seem to be without promise. Such intercessions should tell the truth. That is, they should be truly intercessions, naming real needs in expectation and hope before God. They should not be little sermons about ourselves or to ourselves, cast as prayers. This is a moment for truth and for hunger. For in hearing this word, we are invited to taste the One of whom we have heard, bearing these gifts away in mission.

The table

The meal of Christ's gift is essential in Christian worship.

This assertion ought also be seen as true in the principal Sunday and festival gatherings of the communities of Christianity. In fact, for a variety of reasons the meal has shrunk, no longer to be recognized as a meal in many places, eaten only by the leaders in others, or disappearing altogether on many Sundays in others. Without having to assign blame or sort out the complicated histories of these developments, it is clear for us that such evidence as we may garner from the New Testament churches, from the early centuries of the church, and from the first years of the Reformation, indicates that from very early on Christians regarded every *Lord's Day* as the occasion for the *Lord's Supper*. Thus, the community at Troas gathers "to break bread" on the first day of the week (Acts 20:7). The first or second century community of the writing called the *Didache* is exhorted to "come together, break bread and hold Eucharist" on the Lord's Day (*Didache* 14:1). The Lutheran churches of the early sixteenth century confess that "in our churches mass is celebrated every Sunday and on other festivals" (*Apology of the Augsburg Confession*, 24:1).

But the recovery of full participation in the holy supper as the principal service of every Christian community on every Sunday remains the goal of many, not simply because of historical or theological wisdom, though these are not to be ignored. Rather, it is because we need it. We need the meal side-by-side with the scriptures in order to understand what the scriptures are about. We need to hear "This is my body" and "This is the new covenant in my blood" in order to encounter Jesus Christ in truth. We need to receive those repeated words "for you" and the gifts they accompany in order to believe and to live in the all-encompassing forgiveness they convey. We need to continually practice word next to meal, meal after word, in order for any newcomers—and the constant "newcomer" in us all—to see what Christianity itself is about, let alone what any Sunday is about: not just ideas and words, but the very presence and mercy of Jesus Christ. We need to be continually formed into "one bread" with all the little, hungry ones of the world who belong to Christ.

The meal of Christ's gift is one of the essentials of Christian worship, especially on every Sunday and festival.

The *meal*? Is it really a meal, this broken bit of bread, this sip of wine? Yes. In fact, the supper of the Lord is made up of the old beginning of a Jewish meal (when God was blessed and thanked over a loaf of bread that was then shared) together with the old end of such a meal (when God was praised at length over a cup of wine that was then shared around the table to conclude the gathering). In the earliest Christian churches, this bread and cup still framed a full meal. But over the first century of Christian life, the food, which continued to be brought to the gathering of the church, or the money, which was brought to purchase food, came to be given away.

This may be because persecution forced the common meal to be held in the morning rather than at supper time. Or it may be that Christians came to concur with Paul's criticism of the factions and favoritism which could occur at such a "church supper" as inappropriate to the meal that proclaims Christ's death (1 Cor. 10–11). In any case, the resulting shape of the supper was a new kind of meal: one that could be eaten by many people at once; one wherein thanks were said over the bread and the wine, these being the very signs filled with Christ's gift of himself; and one where much food and money were still brought but, except for the loaf and the cup, all of it was given away to the hungry.

The mid-second-century writer Justin goes on immediately after his description of the gathering for scripture reading, preaching, and prayer, to describe the Sunday gathering of Christians:

> When we have concluded the prayer, bread is set out to eat, together with wine and water. The presider likewise offers up prayer and thanksgiving, as much as he can, and the people sing out their assent saying the "amen." There is a distribution of the things over which thanks have been said and each person participates, and these things are sent by the deacons to those who are not present. Those who are prosperous and who desire to do so, give what they wish, according to each one's choice, and the collection is deposited with the presider. He aids orphans and widows, those who are in want through disease or through another cause, those who are in prison, and foreigners who are sojourning here. In short, the presider is a guardian to all those who are in need. We hold this meeting together on the day of the sun since it is the first day, on which day God, having transformed darkness and matter, made the world. On the same day Jesus Christ our Savior rose from the dead . . . he appeared to his apostles and disciples and taught them these things which we have presented also to you.
> (1 *Apology*, 67)

Such a collection of food and money belongs essentially to the Christian meal and is one source of our continued practice of taking a collection on Sunday (cf. 1 Cor. 16:2).

So, this meal is a *meal* because it is a loaf to eat together and a cup to drink together, because it is accompanied by a meal prayer, because it longs for a feast for the poor, and because, in all of this, it tastes of God's mercy.

But then, just as with the "word," the "table" of Christian worship practice is made up of two things together, pressing us toward a third. In the "table," thanksgiving is set next to eating and drinking, and these two together press us toward collection and toward mission.

Food is set out. Not just any food, but a loaf of bread, which is widely seen as the principal staple food in human communities and which connects to Jesus' meals, and wine, which is widely seen as the principal festive drink in human communities and which also connects to Jesus' meals. In some places of the world, because of the scarcity of bread and/or wine and because of the great need to show that this gift of Christ is always a local, contemporaneous gift, some other staple food or festive drink may need to be used. But in North America, our need will be this: to let it be seen that the bread is really bread and that there is a full cup of wine available for all.

And thanks are given. That is, a single leader—usually the person who is presiding in the liturgy, usually, in fact, the same person who brought the scripture readings to living voice in the preaching—*proclaims the praise of God over the bread and cup, doing so with the full assent and the active participation of the whole assembly.* We all, standing around, respond with ancient responses, sing out refrains and the song of the angels; we say "amen." This thanksgiving proclaims the promise of God present to all the world in Jesus Christ. It celebrates that God has created all things and invites all to taste that creation restored in Jesus Christ. It laments deep pains and losses, even death, yet it trusts that this very food of Christ is a foretaste of the times when God will wipe away all tears. At the heart of the thanksgiving, the very words Christ speaks at the supper are proclaimed, inviting all to hear and see what the meal is for and who is the true host. Because of the centrality of this thanksgiving, the entire meal and indeed the entire word-meal service is sometimes called *eucharist*, from the old Greek-Christian word for thanksgiving to God through Christ.

The thanksgiving prayer, in whatever form it takes, gives words to the eating and the drinking which follow. But the eating and drinking receive a gift greater than any prayer can proclaim: Here, by the power of the Spirit and the word of promise, is the very *encounterable self* of Jesus Christ—his body—and the very *life* of Jesus poured out as the promised new covenant—his blood. *All who are present who belong to that body are given to eat and drink, and the food is sent to those who are absent.* With Christ, then, there come to all the nations, to all outsiders, to us, all the riches and treasures, all the grace, all the judgment but also all the mercy of God.

Yet the world is still hungry. Judgment unrelieved by mercy seems to be everywhere. Death seems the most final lot. Thus, the liturgy has helped us to speak these truths. So we have taken a collection, to make a little dent in the sorrow, to help a few, to bear witness to Christ among the poor. We do this because Christ has gathered all the sorrow into himself and now testifies that God's promise is finally for all the world. Then we quickly leave, on mission to live out our hope amid the conditions of the world, to act out some of the justice for which we have prayed, to turn toward our neighbor with the same love and solidarity which has been shown to us.

Of course, there are disagreements among Christians about what the presence of the body and blood of Jesus really means, and some of these

18

disagreements are serious. There are also disagreements about what to call the meal, about the exact food which should be used, about the form of the thanksgiving, about the manner of distribution, and about who precisely should eat and drink. This assertion that the meal is central and is to be held every Sunday is not meant to circumvent the serious discussion which still needs to be held among many Christians in the hope of finding sufficient common ground to enable the richer fellowship of their churches. Even so, these disagreements should not distract us from the centrality of this biblical gift nor from the urgent though neglected role it plays in many of our diverse traditions. In spite of the disagreements, Christ has given us the supper *in common.*

These things, then, belong to the supper: thanksgiving and eating and drinking. These things together urge us toward mission.

Word and table is the pattern of Sunday and festival worship. It is the pattern of scripture readings and preaching (leading to intercessions) followed by thanksgiving and eating and drinking (accompanied by a collection and sending us away). But must it be in this order? Could it be table followed by word or preaching followed by scriptures? The logic of the ancient order is simple and clear and it is hard to see why one would choose to change it, except to somewhat dubiously demonstrate one's own independence. Indeed, when set in the midst of a needy world, the order can be seen to follow a pattern which ought not be changed: The words of scripture and preaching lead us to speaking words in prayer on behalf of our neighbor and all the world. They also awaken in us a hunger and thirst for the taste of God's goodness. But the supper sends us away to be the body of Christ to our neighbor, to be for our neighbor what we have received in the supper.

The bath

Christian worship includes that washing by which persons are added to the community of Christ.

This "baptism," as the bath is called by all Christians, belongs to Sunday. The Sunday gathering of Christians may actually include such a baptism of a new Christian, at the same time giving all those who have gathered the occasion to be renewed once again in baptismal meaning themselves. Or, the Sunday assembly of Christians may include some act or acts of the return to baptism—simply walking past the water-pool on the way into the gathering; confession and forgiveness by the water; the sign of the cross; a baptismal hymn or psalm together with the scattering of water; the confession of the baptismal creed; prayer for those coming to be baptized.

Modern evangelical practice has urged us to set a strong remembrance of baptism and a gracious clarity about the way one comes to baptism in every Christian gathering, in order to invite and welcome the puzzled newcomer, to have available the deepest possible response to the newcomer's inquiry about God and grace. Furthermore, the increasingly widespread ecumenical practice discourages baptizing people in private, in purely family rites, as a contradiction of the very meaning of baptism. The washing needs to take place in the community. Even in cases of emergency, more and more churches try to assemble as many people from the community as possible to assist with the washing. Current liturgical practice has urged us to consider using the great festivals of the year—Easter, especially, but also Pentecost and Epiphany—as primary times for baptizing, thereby making the return of those festivals each year into a return of baptismal meaning. Even our funerals have something of the water in them: the body set near the font or under the great garment of baptism or near the great candle, and baptismal texts spoken or sung as grounds for the promise of life in the midst of death.

Then, what is this bath, that it should be so central? Isn't it simply the way we start someone out on the Christian life? Yes, but it is far more than that. Or, rather, in our beginning, made by God, is already hidden all the realities of our middle and our end, of our full life, of our death and of our life in God. In our beginning is not just our *selves*, but ourselves held in Christ's hands together with all those who belong to the church. We need to see these things more clearly in the ways we celebrate baptism. The church is to make a great deal of this beginning—for every child and for every adult coming fresh to the community.

Baptism is a washing with water in the name and by the command of Jesus Christ, such that the one who is washed is joined to Christ, under the Spirit of God, before the face and voice of God, in the company of all the church. Every baptism participates in the meaning of the stories of the baptism of Jesus himself (Mark 1:9-11 and parallels): The candidate goes into the water with Christ, the Spirit hovers, and the voice of the Father calls this one a beloved child. Such is baptism "in the name of the Father and of the Son and of the Holy Spirit" (Matt. 28:19). Every baptism participates in the meaning of the stories of the death and resurrection of Christ, his final "baptism" (Mark 10:38; Luke 12:50). Using the poetic language of the church, we may say that every baptism is God hovering over the water, creating the world anew; Noah and the people with Noah and all the animals surviving the flood; the people coming across the sea to freedom; water springing from the rock in the desert; the world renewed with living water; the womb of the church giving birth.

Washing with water in order to be ready for God already existed in the time of Jesus' ministry. In various ways, washings were part of the religious movements for renewal which marked the Judaism of the time of Christian origins, movements we know best by the New Testament evidence of John the Baptist's baptisms. Just as with the reading of scriptures in an assembly and the eating of a meal as a prayer, this washing was also taken by Jesus and his followers to be done in a new way as a means for proclaiming the grace of God. Only now, Christians were not to wash repeatedly, hoping to be pure for God's coming. Nor did they enact a washing, saying that "someone" unknown was coming. They were washed in Jesus' name, they were washed *once*, thereby joining the community which believed that the hoped-for day of God's coming had already begun in Jesus' death and resurrection.

It is this washing which we still do. Paradoxically, we have sometimes let the practice of the washing "shrink" into a smaller deed of less consequence. Some have seen baptism as essentially a thing done to babies, a passage rite at birth to launch the child into life. Others have regarded it as an option, useful to express one's decision for faith. But the deep human longing for God to really come, for justice to occur, for tears to be wiped away is still alive in us. The recovery of a vigorous baptismal practice is about this ancient longing. The water-washing and the teaching which leads to the water-washing and the constant return to the water-washing all mean to say: God is with us. God comes into the most God-forsaken places, the places summed up in Jesus' cross. The wiping away of tears has begun in the resurrection, and that beginning is washed over us in baptism.

As with "word" and "table," "bath" is also made up of two things. There is the water and there is the name. Christian baptism is made up of *water*, as much water as possible, poured over the candidate as a gift of life and grace. At the same time, Christian baptism is the *teaching* about God, about God's grace, about God known in Jesus, about the mercy of the holy Trinity. That word and teaching is the "name" of God, God's own self and power encountered and called upon. Such teaching leads to the font. It is discussed between candidates and sponsors and teachers on the way to the font. It is gathered up in the "catechism," the things learned in the baptismal process—the commandments, the creed, the prayer of Jesus, the words spoken in the sacraments, the way of return to baptism through absolution. This teaching is returned to throughout life.

The two things of baptism—the name and the water—press us toward a third: toward community with each other. That is, toward reminding each other of these things, toward communally bearing witness to the grace of God in the world.

Both the font and the name need to be unshrunk in our practice. The name in which we baptize needs to be much more than a formula or a rote confession of faith. Our churches will do well to recover a process of formation and teaching which leads to baptism and flows from baptism for both adult and infant candidates. We need sponsors, mentors or godparents, catechists or teachers, pastors, and members of the local community who take with great seriousness their roles in accompanying those who are being baptized. We need to help each other be less afraid to speak about God and grace to those who have begun to be curious about the hope that is in us. And we need to let the washing itself be a powerful event, mirroring in the force of its symbol and ritual the consequence of its meaning. We need to make our pools larger, when we can. We need to wash our candidates, clothe them, anoint them, give them burning lights, sign them with the cross, lead them into the assembly, give them the holy food to eat and drink, talk with them of what has happened to them, think with them of what we shall do together now to bear witness to God's mercy in the world.

Of course, there are disagreements among Christians about baptism, too. Shall we only baptize believers or are the infant children brought by believers to be candidates as well? Must the washing include a full submersion or is pouring or even sprinkling enough? But, once again, even these disagreements ought not distract us from the astonishing gift, the sign of God's new age, which we have been given in common.

In fact, the disagreement about "believers' baptism" can push us all deeper, towards renewal. The ecumenical statement on *Baptism, Eucharist & Ministry* proposes:

> In order to overcome their differences, believer baptists and those who practice infant baptism should reconsider certain aspects of their practices. The first may seek to express more visibly the fact that children are placed under the protection of God's grace. The latter must guard themselves against the practice of apparently indiscriminate baptism and take more seriously their responsibility for the nurture of baptized children to mature commitment to Christ. (*BEM*: "Baptism," 16)

Thus, the tasks for believer baptist groups are seeing that grace is indeed operative in baptism and regarding the children of believers as, in some sense, enrolled candidates for baptism, the washing itself to be enacted as they grow in years. The tasks for infant baptizers involve welcoming a serious process for forming and teaching the baptized in discipleship and faith. For both, unshrinking the name will help.

So will unshrinking the font, though if we are tempted to argue with each other about how much water we use, we may be helped by reading the wonderful first or second century text of the *Didache:*

> Concerning baptism, baptize thus: Having rehearsed all these things [the nascent catechism], baptize in the name of the Father and of the Son and of the Holy Spirit, in running water; but if you have no running water, baptize in other water, and if you cannot in cold, then in warm. But if you have neither, pour water three times on the head. (*Didache*, 7:1-3)

As much water as possible is ideal. But there is no requirement; there is only grace. Yet that is no excuse for minimalism, as if God would be pleased if we did less, spoke less, used less. It is *we* who need the washing of the water and the teaching of the name in stronger forms.

Centrality and mode of celebration

So these are the essentials of Christian worship: A community *gathers in prayer* around the scriptures *read* and *preached*. This community of the word then tastes the meaning of that word by keeping the meal of Christ, *giving thanks* over bread and cup and *eating* and *drinking*. It is this word-table community, the body of Christ, which gathers other people to its number, continually *teaching* both itself and these newcomers the mercy and mystery of God and *washing* them in the name of that God. All of these essential things urge the community toward the world—toward prayer for the world, sharing with the hungry of the world, caring for the world, giving witness to the world.

Around these central things, which will be most evident in Sunday and festival worship, other gatherings of Christians may also take place. *Like planets around the sun, these other gatherings will reflect the light of the central Sunday gathering.* They will do so mostly by repeating and echoing the readings, the songs, the prayers, and the blessings of the Sunday assembly. Or these other gatherings will be intended to help inquirers, newcomers, and candidates for baptism to come more deeply into the mystery which is at the heart of the Sunday assembly: reading and discussing the scriptures with them, praying for them. Both sorts of Christian gatherings—daily prayer and "seeker services" or "catechumenal gatherings"—will come to their purpose most clearly as they are turned toward the full Christian assembly around the essential things.

There are certain dangers in talking about the *essentials* of Christian worship. For one thing, people may forget what they are *for*, *why* they are essential. A church may begin to think that simply to read the scripture and have a sermon is enough, for *whatever* purpose these are done: ideological training, self-realization, the attempt to please God. Or a community may begin to give formal thanks and do the eating and drinking for a variety of skewed reasons: to ensure a good crop, to sanctify a government, to heighten the solidarity of a particular racial or sexual or economic group. Or the washing and naming of God may take place simply to mark a birth as a rite of passage. Or any one of these things may be forced on people, in ways utterly devoid of the love to which the things themselves bear witness.

No. The *reasons* for these essential things belong to their essential character. Word, table, and bath occur at the heart of a participating community so that all people may freely encounter God's mercy in Christ, that they may come to faith again and again, that they may be formed into a community of faith, that they may be brought to the possibility of love for God's world. When these reasons are not manifest in the exercise of the central actions themselves, the deep meaning of the essential things is obscured and betrayed. Even so, God acts in these things. Where we have kept the holy things most dead and deadly, fire can still leap out into the hearts and lives of the assembly. The combination of the liberating words of scripture with the gracious actions given by Christ can yield faith.

The other great danger of speaking about the *essentials* of Christian worship is that we will take such speech as minimalist counsel: Do only such things as will barely count to meet the "essential" requirements. No. The word *essential* here is intended to mean just the opposite. *Let these things be central.* Let them stand at the center, large and full, influencing and determining all else we do. Let the scripture reading be done as if it were clearly the first reason we have come together at all. Let the preaching be more serious, more profound, more gracious. Let the prayers be truly intercessions, the real naming of human need. Let the meal be held every Sunday. Let the food be clearly food. Let the hungry be always remembered. Let the thanksgiving be beautiful and strong. Let the whole assembly eat and drink. Let both the font and the name be "unshrunk."

There remain, of course, a hundred open questions. With what music shall we do these things? With what leadership? Shall our assembly be informal or formal? Shall there be books in our hands, so that a rich variety of written texts can be employed? Or shall the words be simple, known by heart, and the music a refrain or call-and-response, with a choir leading us? How shall these central things be enacted so that they are seen to be hospitable to a diversity of cultures? What shall be the spatial configuration of our assembly? How, exactly, will we gather around the word, the table, and the water-pool? Shall our gathering together, our entry, be slow and intentional or direct and to the point?

The very centrality of bath, word, and table, and the very reasons for their centrality, while not determining absolute answers to these and many other questions, do begin to give us some characteristics of the mode of our celebration. These characteristics, while not exactly essentials, are corollaries which ought not be easily ignored. A list of such characteristics should include *ritual focus*, a *music which serves*, the importance of *Sunday* and other festivals, a *participating community*, *many ministries*, and a *recognized presider* who is in communion with the churches.

In classical Reformation theology, most of these characteristics have been considered to belong to *adiaphora*, the things which are indifferent, the things which are *not* essential. Our relationship with God rests on none of these things. But one should be careful with *adiaphora*. It is not that one can do whatever one likes with these matters, even leaving them out altogether. There will be secondary matters in any Christian service. Rather, one must ask how they are arranged, so as to disclose and assist the things that are primary.

For instance, many kinds of songs or ritual may make up the flow of the service. But it will need to be clear that the flow of the meeting is *into* and *out of* the central things. A choir anthem or a drama which does not serve the assembly's gathering in the word—which, indeed, turns what was a participating assembly into an audience, alienating them from their own event—is as great a problem now as it was in the Middle Ages. We will need to keep asking about style and music, about how we gather, but these questions will always need to be balanced with an inquiry about whether our answers are helping people to do the essential things or are distracting them.

Music is a case in point. Many sorts of music can and have served the Christian community. This creative development should continue. But music that exalts the performer and silences the community, music that has no room for the whole assembly's voice, music that is marked only by despair or only by happiness—these will have much difficulty serving the gathering around the central matters. Indeed, that whole gathering, at its best, is musical—with its variety of voices, its rhythms and resolutions. It will be good if the musical character of the assembly is always coming to expression in actual music, new and old. But this music will have to *serve*, turning its power to evoke and to gather toward the needs of the people as they sing around word, bath, and table, and letting the primary role of the choir be to lead this people. The creation of a liturgical music—a *pastoral* music—is a necessary task in every era and every culture.

While we have not listed Sunday or certain festivals among the essentials of Christian worship, it should be clear that Sunday matters a great deal to Christians. So do Easter and the cycle of days that lead to and from Easter. These days ought not be set aside unless for a very serious reason. Since the essential things of Christian worship are those things which gather us into Christ, it is clear *why* Sunday and the principal festivals matter: They are about Christ. Every Sunday proclaims that the God who made the world has raised Jesus up. Sunday, then, is properly the day for assembly around the very things—word and table—which regularly show this resurrection to us. Easter is a kind of Sunday to the year. Christians can and do gather on other days. All days are holy; none are closer to God. But as long as the Gospels are read, Sunday will have priority as the day of Christian assembly.

Assembly—that word has been used repeatedly here. Again, the word *worship* could mislead us into thinking that we are talking about ways that Christians may privately praise God and that the gathering of Christians is simply a collection of those private ways in one room. In fact, the classic Christian approach to worship has gone in just the other direction. I need the community in order to hear that word of grace and life—on the lips of my sister or brother and of all those gathered—that word which I cannot make up for myself or speak to myself. I need the assembly to be baptized and to remind me of my baptism. I need the community to celebrate the supper. "Assembly" is not adiaphoral in Christian worship. Of necessity, it may be a very small assembly: the gathering of Christians in the room of someone sick or dying, for example. But we cannot do without it. These essential things belong essentially in the open, public assembly of Christians. Then my private prayer recalls these things, turns them over in my heart, rehearses them, repeats them before God: "These things I remember, as I pour out my soul: how I went with the throng and led them in procession to the house of God" (Psalm 42:4).

But such a gathering is not a collective, not a crowd, not a mob, not a cheering section. In a Christian gathering each person should be welcomed, each person respected for their baptismal dignity or for the mystery God made in them. Each person's gifts are to be brought in ways that serve the assembly's purpose, each person is to be addressed with love. There should be space, hospitality, respect, silence, room for one's own thoughts, no compulsion, no forcing of people to recite texts they have never seen and do not believe. This is a *personal* communal gathering.

And it is a participating assembly. By the songs and actions that surround the central things it should be evident that *we* gather for the word, *we* enact the bath, *we* hold the supper. But it will come to focused expression when from the baptized people assembled here, various people are drawn to minister in love to the assembly: doorkeepers, musicians, cantors and the rehearsed voices of the choir, readers of scripture, a leader of the intercessions, bringers of gifts, ministers of communion and those chosen to bear the bread and cup away to the absent, catechists, sponsors. The repeated juxtapositions of two things which make up the essence of Christian worship—scripture readings next to preaching, thanksgiving next to sharing the food, teaching next to the bath—will be more clearly manifest if different persons are heard reading the scripture, distributing the food, helping with the teaching. Certainly, we can do the essential things without these offices being filled, with only one ordained leader, for example. But the fuller expression of the central things, a celebration which accords with their meaning, calls for these ministries.

Neither can we do without a presider. Some churches regard a presider who is ordained as one of the essentials of Christian worship. Other churches take such leadership for granted, doing the ordinations but hesitating to call this essential lest one miss the word, table, and font this presider is called upon to serve. This is not the place for that debate. It can only be asserted here that the agreement is greater than is ordinarily seen. When the ministry of the presider is placed where it belongs—in the participating assembly around the essential things—there is an astonishing concurrence on the need for such a leader: to speak the lively word in response to the readings or to see that such a word is spoken; to pray at table; and to preside over the process that leads to and through the water. The ministry of the presider is abused and misformed if, rather than serve the people around these central things, it calls attention to itself, to the importance and personality of the minister. There is also a widespread agreement on the need for such a local leader to be in a wider communion, to be one of the local symbols of this community's connection to all the other churches. There remains a disagreement between Christians about the nature and meaning of this wider connection.

These assertions about the nature of Christian worship generally do not mean to deny that there is such a thing as *Lutheran* worship or *Anglican* worship or *Roman Catholic* worship or *Methodist* worship. Lutheran liturgy, for example, treasures hymnody as a nearly essential part of its gatherings and will often repeat the paradox that while *we* do all the good things of the liturgy, it is finally God who is the actor. Roman Catholic worship treasures the patterns of the ancient Roman church as paradigmatic, always seeking to translate those patterns, as they are represented today by the Latin books called the "typical editions," into new situations and new languages.

Different Christian churches rightly try to order their liturgical life around the essentials of worship. At the same time, particular communions manifest a distinctive liturgical style by emphasizing many secondary or nonessential matters.

The differences between the forms of worship are less great than we usually think. Or when they *are* great, we need to ask ourselves if they are obscuring the essentials. Lutheran worship at its deepest—and this is true of all western and eastern Christian worship, as well—is this: a participating assembly, served by its ministers, gathered around the word, the table, and the bath which speak and show Jesus Christ so that the nations may live.

It is these essential things that we all, together, need.

Having said that, can we now ask how to make these things clearer and stronger in our own worship traditions, in our multicultural patterns, in ways new and old? Can we investigate what these essential things have to do with evangelism and with justice? Can we proceed with the open questions?

ABOUT THE AUTHOR

Gordon W. Lathrop is Schieren Professor of Liturgy at Lutheran Theological Seminary in Philadelphia. Among numerous published works, his most recent is *Holy Things: A Liturgical Theology* (Fortress, 1993). He is the general editor of *Open Questions in Worship.*

RESPONSES
Ruth A. Meyers

Christian worship means more than calling upon Christ. We proclaim the word and celebrate baptism and eucharist not only because Jesus commanded his disciples to do so. We do them because in them Christ is present, because in them the assembly encounters the living Christ, because in them we participate in Christ.

Jesus promised his disciples: "Where two or three are gathered in my name, I am there among them" (Matt. 18:20). After his death and resurrection, the disciples experienced his presence when they gathered for the breaking of bread (cf. Luke 24:35). The apostle Paul described the bread and the cup as a sharing in the body and blood of Christ (1 Cor. 10:16).

It is important to recognize that Christ's presence is not limited to the bread and wine. Christ is present in the whole celebration of word and sacrament. It is Christ who speaks in the proclamation of scripture. The assembly is the body of Christ, the people of God gathered in the name of Christ, incarnate in a particular time and place. Christ is represented in the minister who baptizes and who presides over the word and the table.

Moreover, the presence of Christ is not static, but it is a dynamic transforming experience. The totality of Christian worship—the proclamation of the word, the baptismal washing, the holy supper—is a saving encounter with Christ. We meet the living Christ, not merely the memory of one who lived, died, and rose nearly two thousand years ago. Thus, we are empowered to be Christ in the world. The potential for transformation, for conversion, is always present. The Spirit may act in our hearts in ways we do not immediately recognize. The grace and mercy of God may wash over us in ways so subtle we are scarcely aware of the changes occurring.

The actions of worship

Understanding worship as an encounter with Christ suggests another significant dimension: Worship calls for the active participation of the people. Lathrop emphasizes that the essentials of worship are actions. More specifically, they are the actions of a community engaged in its encounter with the living Christ. The participation of the congregation is essential because it is the congregation who participates in Christ. The words, songs, gestures, actions, even silences express and enact the encounter with Christ that is so central to worship.

27

The use of symbols

Of especial importance in worship are the primary symbols: bread, wine, water. Christ is present in concrete, tangible elements, and our worship ought to use these elements in ways that express the abundance of God's blessing. A significant part of the twentieth-century renewal of worship has been a fuller use of these central symbols. The ordinary elements of water, bread, and wine allow us to encounter Christ in ways readily accessible to our senses. *We meet Christ not in some abstract spiritual way, but in these very tangible substances that by their use in worship permeate the very core of our being.* An expansive use of these symbols helps us glimpse the infinite, incomprehensible, overflowing love of God in Christ Jesus.

The relation of bath, word, and table

The celebration of baptism not only includes washing in the name of the triune God, but in its fullness begins with the proclamation of the word and is the entrance into the eucharistic community. In some churches the celebration of baptism concludes with the eucharistic meal: Word, bath, and table are held together in one primal encounter with Christ. Other celebrations of word and table bring us back to the original celebration of baptism. The weekly proclamation of the word echoes the teaching leading up to the font. Participation in the holy supper reunites us with the Christ we encountered in baptism. The weekly meal is the ongoing expression of baptismal participation in Christ. Word and table always plunge us into the same reality into which we are baptized, the reality of the creative and redemptive love of God made known in Jesus.

Worship and Christian living

United with Christ through word and sacrament, we are sent forth into the world to be the body of Christ. Lathrop tells us that the essentials of Christian worship lead us onward to respond to the needs of the world.

The ecumenical document *Baptism, Eucharist & Ministry* describes the implications of the eucharist in this way:

> All kinds of injustice, racism, separation, and lack of freedom are radically challenged when we share in the body and blood of Christ. Through the eucharist the all-renewing grace of God penetrates and restores human personality and dignity. The eucharist involves the believer in the central event of the world's history. As participants in the eucharist, therefore, we prove inconsistent if we are not actively participating in this ongoing restoration of the world's situation and the human condition. (*BEM*: "Eucharist," 20)

In the eucharist, in word and table, we encounter the all-embracing love of God. We come to know the one who casts down the mighty and lifts up the lowly, who fills the hungry with good things but sends the rich away empty. We discover God's yearning for us, a yearning so great that God took on human flesh and lived as one of us.

Ruth A. Meyers is Diocesan Liturgist in the Episcopal Diocese of Western Michigan and an associate faculty member at Ecumenical Theological Seminary in Detroit, Michigan.

John Ferguson

What is truth? What is biblical truth? Lathrop writes that at worship scripture is "read so that the community may encounter the truth about God in Jesus Christ enlivened by the living Spirit." He is not alone in proposing that the issue of revealed truth is at work when we gather for worship. In a recent interview, Frederick Buechner quotes Karl Barth as saying that everybody comes to church with the question, "Is it true, is it true?"

In the summer of 1994, a conference was held at St. Olaf College called "Reclaiming the Bible for the Church." The presenters at this gathering proposed that over the years the "right" to interpret the Bible has passed from the church to the academy (scholars at work primarily in seminaries, colleges, and universities). When the academy was peopled by believers, this was a helpful and good practice. More recently, when some members of the academy became suspicious of faith, the academy still maintained its place as the voice of biblical interpretation. The presenters at this conference proposed that the church must reclaim its responsibility to interpret the Bible for the world. If the Bible is the word of God for God's people, the church must reclaim its responsibility and right to preach and teach the Bible from the wisdom of the church as church, from a position of faith.

If indeed, the church needs to assume responsibility for the teaching and interpretation of the Bible, and if Lathrop is correct in suggesting that worship is the primary way most people encounter the biblical message, then what truth we tell, what message we send to those who worship becomes a critical issue. Lathrop tells us that as we worship we are reminded of who we are as the people of God; we tell and teach newcomers the meaning and mystery of God. Yet at the same time we are facing a complete paradigm shift as the church struggles to define its role in this post-Christian era now upon us.

All of this change and instability can have a profound impact on levels buried deeply within us. The tensions of our time, the challenges to our faith can be so subtly at work that we don't even recognize their impact upon our lives and the choices we make. It is indeed tempting to look for the quick solution, to sell out to the values of the world, often without realizing that such a sellout has taken place. For instance, the biblical notion of success is certainly not in harmony with our culture's notion of success. If the Bible is untrue, then we are only left with models of success affirmed by our contemporary culture. The successful church will be defined not by biblical models, but by contemporary ones. Growth is a contemporary measure of success in which the ends (growth) justify the means (abandoning the essentials of worship as Lathrop describes them).

What does one do? Each person has to wrestle with these issues and determine how best to proceed. Right now I must affirm that I cannot serve as a church musician using styles that sometimes can make the message appear superficial and transient. Yet, I do want to be sensitive to the needs of others, aware that their notions of appropriate music for worship may be different from mine. Indeed, I hope to work toward a kind of worship music that Lathrop describes. A music that invites all to join in the song. A music that incorporates a great variety of styles and traditions. A music that relates to people of differing backgrounds. A music that reminds us all that the song of God's people has been sung over the centuries—a song that is not ours alone because it is a part of God's grace-filled gift of salvation that is offered to all.

To serve God's people, to lead their song, is an enormous challenge. It has always been so. It is never easy and has never been easy to find the way. Yet with the guidance of the living Spirit, the way will be found so that "through the Church, the song goes on."

John Ferguson is Elliot and Klara Stockdal Johnson Professor of Organ and Church Music and Cantor to the Student Congregation at St. Olaf College, Northfield, Minnesota.

FOR FURTHER READING

For a general introduction to the essentials:
Baptism, Eucharist & Ministry. Faith and Order Paper No. 111. Geneva: World Council of Churches, 1982.

Lathrop, Gordon. *Holy Things: A Liturgical Theology.* Minneapolis: Fortress, 1993.

Willimon, William H. *Word, Water, Wine, & Bread: How Worship Has Changed over the Years.* Valley Forge: Judson, 1980.

For children and their parents about the essentials:
Ramshaw, Gail. *Sunday Morning.* Chicago: Liturgy Training Publications, 1993.

From an Episcopal perspective:
Mitchell, Leonel L. *The Meaning of Ritual.* Ridgefield, Connecticut: Morehouse Publishers, 1991.

From a Lutheran perspective:
Brand, Eugene. *The Rite Thing.* Minneapolis: Augsburg, 1970.

Vajta, Vilmos. *Luther on Worship.* Philadelphia: Fortress, 1958.

From a Methodist perspective:
Stookey, Lawrence Hull. *Eucharist: Christ's Feast with the Church.* Nashville: Abingdon, 1993.

From an Orthodox perspective:
Schmemann, Alexander. *For the Life of the World.* New York: St. Vladimir's Seminary Press, 1974.

From a Roman Catholic perspective:
Guardini, Romano. *Sacred Signs.* Wilmington: Michael Glazier, 1979.

Searle, Mark. *Liturgy Made Simple.* Collegeville: The Liturgical Press, 1981.

ANNOUNCING A NEW SUBSCRIPTION SERIES FROM
AUGSBURG FORTRESS . . .

OPEN QUESTIONS IN WORSHIP

Gordon Lathrop, Series Editor

EIGHT VOLUMES
$34.95 (includes shipping and handling)

Subscribe now and receive all eight volumes of *Open Questions in Worship*. Volume 1 will be published in November 1994, and the subsequent seven volumes will be published at quarterly intervals. Subscribers who join the series after November 1994 will receive upcoming volumes as well as all back issues.

Open Questions in Worship explores current issues and emerging practices in the church's worship from a variety of open perspectives. Drawing on the wisdom of pastors, musicians, and liturgical scholars, this new series will assist those who care for the church's worship: clergy, associates in ministry, church musicians, directors of worship, worship planning committees, evangelism committees, Christian/religious educators, altar guilds, adult study groups.

Gordon Lathrop, Schieren Professor of Liturgy at Lutheran Theological Seminary at Philadelphia, is the general editor of *Open Questions in Worship*.

This series includes these volumes:

1. What are the essentials of Christian worship? *Available Nov. 1994*
2. What is "contemporary" worship? *Feb. 1995*
3. How does worship evangelize? *May 1995*
4. What is changing in baptismal practice? *Aug. 1995*
5. What is changing in eucharistic practice? *Nov. 1995*
6. What are the ethical implications of worship? *Feb. 1996*
7. What does "multicultural" worship look like? *May 1996*
8. How does the liturgy speak of God? *Aug. 1996*

To order, call 800-328-4648, ext. 578

Augsburg Fortress
PUBLISHERS